Three Days
in the Life of an
African Christian Villager

Jim Harries

WIPF & STOCK · Eugene, Oregon

Wipf and Stock Publishers
199 W 8th Ave, Suite 3
Eugene, OR 97401

Three Days in the Life of an African Christian Villager
By Harries, Jim
Copyright©2011 by Harries, Jim
ISBN 13: 978-1-5326-7789-2
Publication date 12/20/2018
Previously published by Bright Pen, 2011

Preface

This short fictitious diary over three days of the life of a reflective African man, written by a long-term missionary to Africa, sets out to illustrate aspects of rural village life often not appreciated by Western mission, development agencies and scholarship. While fictitious in its detail, the kinds of events described are very real. This account provides insights in simple prose form into a contemporary non-western way of life that could barely be found in any other way. The author's 23 years of living in rural Africa as part of a village community enable him to communicate at depth with uncanny simplicity by simply relating events and this African man's thoughts about them.

The need for inter-cultural communication, inter-cultural ministry and relationship is all of the rage in our globalising world. So it should be. This simple diary implicitly suggests that important things may sometimes be being missed. In-depth accounts of African ways typically being presented by Africans may not be able to answer questions that are implicit in the minds of Westerners. Few Westerners have a deep and long-term exposure to African village life. Jim Harries sets out in this account to enlighten those interested in the continent of something of the complexities of contemporary life in the hope that this will encourage intervention to be more enlightened, whether in the area of Christian mission, or of encouraging socio-economic development.

These days so-called inter-cultural communication is often practised in English. This little book suggests (implicitly) that the use of English as international language and for brokering 'inter-cultural' relationships may be far from adequate and even counter productive. That is - that English can actually conceal more than it reveals. The use of English as inter-cultural medium of communication can give the person from the non-native English speaking world an appearance of familiarity through their use of this 'global language'. By concealing rather than interacting with difference, the use of a 'global language' may not lead to the formation of effective (mutually comprehensible and transparent) relationships. Cultural differences will remain in a relationship even if they are hidden. They are likely at some point to emerge and quite likely unexpectedly to interfere with what might have seemed a smooth process of relating.

In focus particularly are relationships set up between native English speakers and African people. The people-group here examined, the Luo of western Kenya have been in close contact with the West for over 100 years. The language of formal education and government amongst the Luo is English. The Luo have a reputation for being highly educated. Their good knowledge of English often has Luo people, as also other African people, conceal important aspects of their home and day to day lives in formal and even informal communication with the outside world. Sometimes they may conceal these things intentionally - so as not to be mocked or laughed at, or so as not to communicate on things that the global community anyway cannot understand. Other times aspects of Luo life will simply disappear in the course of translation into English, because equivalent English terms have such a different impact to the Luo originals that a lot of meaning is lost.

Many Luo people would struggle to articulate just which areas of their lives may be strikingly or in important ways foreign to non-Luo people. Those we are here especially concerned for are Westerners. This is why this short booklet has been written by a Westerner, who has lived in a Luo village for an extended period. His experience of day to day life in a Luo community may still be very limited. His understanding of deep Luo thinking will certainly still be minimal by comparison with that of a native Luo. On the other hand, having been born and raised in the West, he may be able to communicate aspects of day-to-day Luo life and thought that a Luo person themselves would not think to or would not consider as important.

This book then represents an attempt by Jim Harries to articulate some of the reflections, thoughts, movements and events that occupy a 'Luo man' in the course of village life over just three 'typical' days. The editors of this book discussed at length whether the original Luo language version of this book should be included with this text. In the end it was thought that there was no point in doing so, because 99% of the target readership would not have and would not be seeking to have any understanding of Dholuo itself. Hence only a few Luo words are retained; those that appear to be particularly difficult to translate into English without causing confusion and loss of meaning. Their meaning (impact) is to be picked up by the reader in the course of reading. (Detailed definitions of terms given in English may be misleading rather than helpful.) The reader should note that this diary is a translation of an original in the Luo language. Translation into English has been carried out as 'literally' as possible so includes a lot of Luo word-order which results (knowingly) in clumsy English that retains grammatical errors.

We welcome the reader to study this text and to ponder on it. I believe that some of the clumsy English used in this translation represents important differences in Luo outlook as against Western English language uses. I believe also that this appreciating of some of the differences in outlook that are reflected in the way language is used and the things that come to be important in this small book is important in our globalising world. Not taking into account people's ways of thinking and communicating while providing them with a veneer of 'foreign understanding' may not be in their best long term interests, or those of the globe.

It is my hope that those Westerners who read this text will be encouraged to expose themselves to African ways of life and languages before intervening in African communities either in mission or in development. Jim Harries is the chairman of the Alliance for Vulnerable Mission - which believes that some Western missionaries should engage in ministry outside of the West through the use of indigenous languages and resources.
(See www.vulnerablemission.org)

Friday

I got up when *piny* (the world, down, country, can also refer to the dead) was still cold. As I stood in my doorway, I saw the houses of my sons lined up below me in the *dala* (homestead). Some on the right, some on the left, as our *dala* we do plan. I began to think about what I saw. The *piny* was cool at that time; but what is *piny*? *Piny* can talk, according to politicians, as '*piny* says' - is the name chosen in Dholuo to translate *serikal* (government). *Piny* (the departed) is those who have already reached below *piny* (the earth). Starting with the people of very long ago. They have died, but they are. They talk, they say, they command, they bless, and they lead. If the *piny* says something, then you must do it.

The *weche* (matters/words) that have us plan our *dala* (homestead) in this way, are of *piny*. These days people *wacho weche* (say things) of *piny* are different to those of God. If it is the *piny* that rules you, you are a person of *piny*. You are not yet saved. You have not yet received the new cleansing that the Whites brought. It is hard for a person to leave the *weche* of *piny* entirely. The *piny* can return him. Our laws tell us, that if the younger son is the first to marry while his brother has not yet married, that is a bad matter/word (*wach*). There are some laws of *piny* that should not be left.

"*Oyawore*", my wife said. "*Oyawore*", I responded. Indeed, it has opened. The darkness is wanting to finish. Light has come into *piny*.

That's the wach we greet with in the morning. That *wach* makes us think of something that was closed but now is not closed. *Piny* has opened up, meaning that light/holy/clean (*ler*) has entered in. We have a *din* (religion/denomination) other around us that are called *Legio Maria*. They can greet people "*Oyawore*" at any time - even at night. They see that the *piny* has opened up, by to the coming of Jesus. The darkness of the *piny* they do see as darkness - as they live in *ler* every day.

The mother of the children went into the kitchen. That's the name I like to call her by. Or, I can call her "daughter of such-and-such a place", according to where she was born. She has lit the fire. The smoke is emerging steadily from under the iron sheets covering the kitchen. The children have already gone into the kitchen to sit with their mother. They have left me to sit alone. They are not very free with me. Even if they want something - it is not easy for them to come to me. They send their mother. A father is someone who is given much respect (fear). Christians like to *lemo* "Our Father, who art in Heaven" - it seems he is also far away from us. He also is the father (owner) of everything. Because *wuon* (father of) anything has power over (is the owner of) that thing.

My shoes are there. They have me fear kneeling (at the front) in the church. Should people see the soles of my shoes, they would realize that poverty is troubling me. Poverty is a very strange *wach*. *Dhier* is the *wach* used to translate the term "poverty" in English. But when we hear that someone is poor, we know he is someone you are amazed at. Maybe you can be amazed because he is wearing two different shoes, or his buttocks are showing through his clothes. That is a person who is *dhier* and you are amazed (*dhiero*) about him (her).

The mother of the children brought the *chai* to the table. These days almost everyone drinks *chai*. Our forefathers would have

2

been amazed with the customs of people who are around today. We despise ourselves. The Whites got us easily. First they gave us sugar for free for us to taste. Once our forefathers had tasted, they found that the sugar was sweet – then they desired it. Then, those people who at first had given us for free wanted money from us! That's how the desires of the flesh direct us.

Long ago we did not know what a 'table' was. A table is part of the civilisation that came just the other day. If you are sitting at a table drinking your *chai* you feel good. If you feel good, well, you are good. When you feel good, you know that there is nothing that can harm you. You have courage. That is one reason why people say - problems have that which brings them. If someone is feeling good, and then *wach* changes and he starts to feel sick, or a friend of his dies, or some other disaster strikes, he knows that cannot happen alone, but there must be someone who has brought it.

I was staying there slowly drinking my *chai*. *Chai* we drink in the house. We can't drink it outside because of *jajuok wang'* (the person with the evil eye). I was startled by another woman's entering the house (family). "Welcome *mama*", I *wach* to her but it seemed as if she had a lot on her mind. Her husband had died the other year. She stays in a bad way. She came in. "*Oyawore*", I greeted her. "*Oyawore*", she greeted me. I did not *lemo*. She did not *lemo*. (Many people these days the thing that they do first on having entered an *ot* (house/family) is *lemo* to God to bless the *ot*. This *mama* but she just came in and started on her *weche* (plural of *wach*).) *Mama* had a lot to complain about. Her eyes moved back and forth. I was startled to find her looking at the table where I was sitting. She stared at the food on the table. Fear took hold of me. I finished the *mandazi* that was in my hand. *Mama* finished what she was doing her *weche* then she left.

The reason that fear took hold of me, is *wach* of the witch with

3

the evil eye. I have heard that people say that this mother bewitches people. There is much jealousy in her heart (liver). If she sees you eating it is easy for her eyes to put something into that food. Then - you get an ailing stomach. The stomach will continue aching until the day you find a *jatak* (witchdoctor to remove the substance from your stomach). *Jatak*'s work is to remove something that is in someone. He can cut you with a razor blade, then he puts his mouth over the cut, and sucks out whatever it is. *Jotak* have helped many people. Many of them are these days found in indigenous churches like of *Roho* (Spirit). I have heard that long ago there were *jonawi*. These are witchdoctors who can pierce you with something. It is said that they liked to pierce girls. Then he (a *janawi*) would force the girl who had been pierced to go and live with that *janawi* (him) in order to have peace. These days they say that saved people cannot get *sihoho* (the disease you get if the evil eye bewitches your food). Myself, I don't entirely agree. Even saved people can get sick.

God (*Nyasaye*) is good, I thought. *Nyasaye* is *wach* in Dholuo made of two words: *nya* and *saye*. Those *weche* show what comes from *sayo* (prayer). Things that *nya* they are many, give birth prolifically, spread profusely. *Sayo* is a way of *lemo* (praying), or asking, so to say *asayi* is like *akwayi*, but *sayo* has more humility than *kwayo*. That is, someone who *sayo* someone else is someone talking to someone senior to them, or imparts to someone seniority. If we put together those two *weche* we get *nyasaye*, meaning the many fruits that are achieved as a result of asking someone (or something) that/who is bigger than you.

Sayo is good. Grabbing stuff without asking, is bad. *Sayo* builds friendship, and relationship, and love. Even if it is also true that, *sayo* is also dangerous. If *sayo* is good, that means also that relationship is good, because if relationship was not good, you wouldn't go and *sayo*. *Nyasaye*, then, is something that arises from relationship, or fellowship that is good – between a person and their fellow person.

Where *nyasaye* is, there is peace. *Nyasaye* is the good thing that emerges from where people relate correctly. It is found in the midst of *sayo* that has consistent humility and relationship-good.

"I *sayi* sir", someone can say, when he reaches his friend, "For you to give me something ... so and so and so ...". It's good if he just gives him. That shows they have a good relationship. Someone who *yako* just takes by force. The fruitfulness, spread and much birth that arises from *nyayako* is not to be found. If someone *sayo* from you something, you can refuse him(her). But refusing him is not good if that thing is there. It is good for you just to agree with him. That is how *nya* arises from *sayo*. If you *sayo* him, if it is possible, then he must give to you. The Bible says, silver and gold - all they are of him *Nyasaye*. So then, if you *lemo* to him in a proper way, he can't refuse you.

Once *piny* was warm enough, I took the time to go and wash. The mother of the children knows how I like the water. She has already taken water in the basin to the bathroom. The bath is outside, so that the sun could shine on me as I washed. I thought about the *wach luokruok* (wash), and the other *wach* that is *lokruok* (repentance/turn around). Those *weche* are very close indeed. The meaning of those *weche* is also close in a way. *Luokruok* means to wash your body for it to be *ler* (clean). *Lokruok* but it means you turn around to be facing in a different way to the way you were originally facing. That is the *wach* that Christians do also to show that they want to leave the ways of *piny* and turn around to be people of God. "Turn around", they can instruct someone.

Then when someone has reached the point of wanting to repent (*lokore*), he usually confesses. Meaning he *wacho weche* (says words) those of sin (or breaking taboo) that are troubling him. The Bible says we should confess with our mouths, so that we rescue our lives (Romans 10:9). Also it says that we should cry out to

God, for him to save us (1 Timothy 2:1). It's coming to the place where people want to take crying out and confessing as important more than repentance (turning around) of the heart ('liver' - *chuny*). Meaning that - many people like to cry out to God, but not to turn around in their way of life.

I carried on washing. My body was getting to be *ler* (clean). That is, *ler* being without dirt or sweat. *Ler* people use in many different ways. All in all we can say that something *ler* is something good. *Ler* is also the power with which the sun chases away darkness. Meaning, it is what you see with. *Ler* shows that there is no uncleanness (*gak*). Someone who is *ler* (holy) is someone who has avoided *richo* (sin/breaking taboo). He (she) does not break taboos. That's why he (she) is *ler*. *Weche* of *richo* have not yet got hold of him/her. That is, it is not easy for illness to get a hold of him. If *wach* like illness takes hold of someone, we know he's not *ler* (holy), or it could be someone has bewitched him/her.

Christians say that God is *ler* (holy). They can repeat that - God is holy, holy, holy. I agree - uncleanness (*chilo*) cannot get a hold on God. A big question though - someone acquires holiness (*ler*) how, and what will being holy (*ler*) do for him? You are holy (*ler*) if you follow the customs and traditions of the Luo as our forefathers knew? Or can someone be holy (*ler*) if he stays close to God? Many people try to be holy by following the law. *Weche* concerning the laws of Moses also easily get mixed up with the laws of our forefathers. If you read the Bible where it says 'laws of long ago', many people know you are talking of the laws of their [Luo] forefathers, but not the laws of God that Moses gave to us.

Once I had washed and dressed it reached the time that I wanted to go to work. I set off. On the way going, I passed many churches. There was a Pentecostal church, another called CCA (Church of Christ in Africa) also known as *johera*. I saw another

6

church that had split-off from CCA that is called *johera-mag-adiera* (CCA-of-Truth). Then I reached the church of Anglican. I was amazed at that name. The real Anglicans from England left them with a name that is adequate for a church that has emerged from under colonialism They called it CPK (Church of the Province of Kenya). But the people of CPK of Kenya did not like that name. They saw it good to be known by the church with whom they were affiliated, so they chose the name of ACK (Anglican Church of Kenya).

The way the different churches worship (*lamo*) varies. Some beat drums. Others do not beat drums. Some clap loudly (hard). Others do not clap, or if they clap then quietly and not loudly. Many of them worship (*lemo*) for a long time - maybe three hours or more. That which all churches have in common – they are seeking for cleansing (*puodhruok*). *Puodhruo*k is what makes *gak* (uncleanness) leave someone. It makes him *ler* in his heart (liver). All in all *puodhruok* cleanses a person from the power of bad ('sinful') *jochiende* (ghosts). These days people like to *wacho* (say) – all *jochiende* are bad (or of sin). People are besmirched by *weche jochiende* of all kinds in the course of life. You can even be besmirched without your knowing. At other times they besmirch you when you know. Besmirchment, or *gak* (uncleanness), or *jochiende* - are adding up during the week. Sunday is the day for removing that besmirchment.

Many people will go to *lemo* (worship) if illness or some problem has taken a hold of them. Meaning when you have already been besmirched a great deal. If someone does not see many troubles, quite likely they won't bother much going to worship. This is what you see every day. People who testify in church many times are giving testimony to how God brought them out of some uncleanness. But it is not the uncleanness (*chilo*) itself that they talk about. It is what that *chilo* brings them, that *lemo* rescues them from; mostly illness or troubles.

If someone goes to church, we say "*odhi lemo*" ("S/he has gone to pray"). He has gone to *lemo* to God. It is only God or gods who you can *lemo* (pray) to. You cannot *lemo* to something else. You cannot say, "I *lemo* you" to a person, for example. Unless you are *lemo* to God for him. *Lemo* again is an amazing word. *Lemo* is a part of the body of a cow or sheep/goats once it has been slaughtered. Meaning – you divide it up *olemo olemo* (piece by piece). Also if the old man wants to die he can divide up his wealth to his sons. That is also *lemo*. He *lemo* to them his wealth.

On the side of the church *lemo* is what you do to/for God, or gods. If you say "I *lemo* for you" to someone then this means you are *lemo* for him for God to help him. You are not asking him for something. *Lemo*, it seems, is that you do so that God be of joy with you. According to Evans-Pritchard, the Nuer people used to *lemo* as they carried out sacrifice. That is, as they slaughtered to God a sheep/goat or cow so that God would bless them. They *lemo* in a way, when everyone is there, so that there be much blessing. *Lemo* is talking with God, but also it carries *wach* many others also – like beseeching, singing, praising, worship, testifying, meeting together, priestcraft (performing ceremonies), etc.

As I was thinking about the *wach* of *lemo* I met a friend of mine. "*Oyawore*", he greeted me. "*Oyawore*", I responded. His name is Omondi. As we wanted to talk, another brother came who is called Olaro. "The Lord be praised", [as said to more person than one] he greeted us. "The Lord be praised", [as said to only one person] we answered him. "The Lord be praised" meaning that the Lord (*ruoth*) should receive praise (*pak*). That is the greetings that saved Christians use to greet one another. It is good if you are a person who loves God that you first think of God when you meet someone before you start talking about things of *piny* (the world/down). Others though do not like greetings like that. They think it is like using the name of God in a way that is not right. It also makes you differentiate in the way you greet between people who are saved and those who are not saved - now it can look as if you are priding yourself over your salvation. "Praise the Lord", people say when they want to be heard. But at times when you want people to hear you, your heart may be far from *weche* about the Lord.

The greetings that people use also vary according to the denomination, in church. We have already said that people of *Legio Maria* like to *wacho oyawore*. *Luong Mogik* (God's Last Appeal Church) *wach* peace (*okue*) or peace [as said to more person than one person] (*okueuru*). Many of the people of the *Roho* churches like to say *murembe* - which is like a *wach* coming from the Luyia language meaning peace.

We greeted him with our hands. Again, we greeted one another while expressing pleasure over having met. We asked one another every person how *wach* is at the *dala* and where he has come from. Once we had known this, my friend Omondi who came first showed me that his senior mother has died, and that she will be buried on the coming Saturday. She has already been taken to the mortuary but the body will be brought to the *dala* on Thursday. He wanted me to know. I was shocked by news of that death. I told him I will come. I must go and stand at that funeral. I can't refuse. People would see me badly if I cannot go and stand at the funeral. The *mama* would haunt me. The Luo know that that departed person sees those who come to the funeral. They give someone who has died much respect (fear).

I thought about another *wach* concerning funerals. That is, the name "*liel*" (funeral) itself. It is the same name as is used for shaving the head of a person. It seems long ago that *liel* was known for this because people would come from it shaven. According to our ancient traditions, people [at a funeral] must be shaved. These days many churches are against that, according to laws that are brought to us in the Old Testament (Deuteronomy 14:1). Others though still go ahead with being shaved. Others again practice shaving of just a little [hair]. They just cut a bit of hair off the head so that *chira* (a curse) should not get them. I don't know if it is right to do that or not? It seems to show that people who do that are still fearing the gods of long ago; they are people who are not fully saved.

Everything else can come to a halt so that the funeral goes on. If someone dies, many people stop work and come from far and wide. They can hang around at a funeral for a long time. Many people carry out burials on Saturday. Now, Fridays and again Sundays vehicles are moving from and to Nairobi taking people to some of the many funerals going on.

On reaching the road, I stood to await a vehicle to carry me. Many vehicles have *weche* of God written on them. One has written on it *"Nyasaye oheri"* (God loves you). What the people of the *matatus* want is money. Getting money for them is hard work. It means getting up early and working till late. It also depends on *hawi* (good fortune). If you don't have *hawi*, you won't be able to get anything. So people of the *matatu* must also search for *hawi*.

Some say that *hawi* is God. You can say to someone *"Hawi* be with you"*. That *wach* is very similar to saying "God be with you". If someone is getting on well in life they say *"Hape* (his *hawi*) is good"*, because he is receiving good things in his life. It looks like for other people their *hawi* is not good. Those who do not have *hawi*, whatever they do does not go well but it goes badly. Your *hawi* is something you can put right through sacrifice. Someone whose *hawi* is bad, if he goes to an *ajuoga* (witchdoctor) he can do things that will rectify his *hawi*.

Something else that resembles *hawi* is *dhoch*. *Dhoch* is something that makes you not to go on in a proper way. *Dhoch* is something that brings illness. *Dhoch* is also something amazing, something that is not right. *Dhoch* can be removed from one person so as to be taken to another person. One day I was in a church that was 'changing' (removing) the *dhoch* from someone. It was a child who was sick. In the church, they had him lie down flat on his back. He close his eyes, and he behaved so as to resemble someone dead. Then the people of that church covered him completely with a white sheet. Then they threw some soil onto the sheet with the boy lying underneath it. When they removed the sheet from him, they knew that the *dhoch* had already left him. They knew that ghost who had brought the illness, if he came to see the child would get lost, realising that the child has died. So then, *dhoch* goes somewhere else. "Changing" (removing) the *dhoch* though, is not good. That is because the *dhoch* does not disappear completely, but goes to take hold of someone else somewhere else.

A *matatu* resembles a place without grace or respect. People are tightly squeezed together in it, everyone sitting very close. If you try and argue with the conductor he cannot hear you. It is just - pure profit! I think at least at times that the above is the case. I think it can be like that because our forefathers did not know *wach matatu*, therefore they could not arrange laws of *matatus*. This means that - *matatus* travel badly.

When we had arrived, I saw that it was time for a cup of *chai*. Next to the road are many *chai*-shacks (called "hotels", but perhaps more accurately "tea-shacks" or "cafés".) They are built in different ways out of different materials. Many of them have earth floors, iron-sheet or mud walls, and iron sheet roofs. One or two tables are in the middle, with a plank of wood supported for people to sit on. The owner of this tea-shack is a lady with many *weche* that she wanted to teach me. She showed me *wach* about choosing a new padre for their church. The padre who was there recently passed away. His death, she said, occurred after it had been prophesied.

One day a lady came, and told people who were preparing for a prior election how *wach* was. She warned people that should they continue to become padres so as to acquire "bigness" in this *piny*, God himself will remove them (from) there. The first padre dies, then the second one died after only three years. If people are not careful, the third one to be newly elected may die quickly. People must "turn around", *lemo* much to God, and leave the lusts of *piny*.

"Whites bring those *weche*", I thought to myself as the *mama* was talking. They are the ones who can agree to give a lot of money into the hands of church leaders. A leader of a church who knows English and who is liked by Whites can become very rich. That is why there can be much jealousy in respect to him. That jealousy kills him, because jealous people must search for a way in which to kill him. That is the foundation to witchcraft. The foundation to witchcraft is jealousy.

[The] *wach* [of] jealousy is very big here in our area. Women who are married in the same home call each other by the name of "my-jealousy" because of this jealousy! Someone who marries more than one woman must be very careful about jealousy indeed. He must do to all his wives the same, so that jealousy not destroy. That is not a *wach* that troubles only homes. Anyone who gets something different from his colleague must be alert. People take each other as loving to put others down. If one person wants to beat his colleagues then there must be others who will want to drag him down again. This is a *wach* that you hear of all the time. This is why someone can be happy when they are the poorest of the poor; no-one will bother dragging him down. It's good to be poor.

In the middle of the day, many people do not eat. People say - they do not have enough money. The truth however is - people are afraid. In the middle of the day, you are together at your place of work. If you eat right there, people must see you. If you go to some other place so as to get food there, they must think that is what you are doing. Someone who carried food from home is considered selfish, unless he shares it out with everyone. But that is difficult. Can you carry enough food for everyone to receive some?

The question now arises as to what to do during your break? Others lie down and sleep. Those who like themselves (are selfish) go and eat. Others though go to hear a preacher. In the middle of the day in the big towns there are preachers who bring *lemo* to people at the times they are resting from their work. Many times they preach outside. Sometimes also in churches. The singers first sing to draw people and excite them. Then the preacher starts his work. The preaching that people like, is of cleansing. That is, you reveal that sin that is there amongst the people. Then you chase that sin away. The love that people have for being cleansed, shows also how they consider themselves to be full of sin. Those who are saved like to be cleansed at any time. That way they see that they will be *ler* all the time. But it is difficult to be *ler* every day. Some other *wach* must enter in. Someone must get sick, and then die. That is why many older people, sick people and those close to death are not taken as having salvation.

When I went back to work, the boss wanted to see me. "New?" he asked me. "Nothing", I answered him. Then "But you are alive?" he asked me. "Indeed, I am alive", I tried to respond. Those two questions were short, but had me think about them later. Why did I respond to tell him that there is "Nothing new"? Why did he ask me that question in the first place? This is what I think - whatever might be new must be bad! So then if you reply "*Onge*", that means that something bad has yet to attack you. Secondly, he asked me if I am alive. But as I was talking to him openly like that - couldn't he see that I am alive? Why has he again asked me about this? The reason is - that someone can be a little bit alive, or a lot alive. If he feels good and is strong, we can say he is "alive completely". If he is sickly or his heart (liver) troubled over something, then he is a little bit alive.

We were almost at the time in which we want to go back to our homes. "Come here (plural) first", the boss told us. We went. The boss told us that the size of our profit was falling. Our income was small. They are concerned - the company could fold. People weren't buying [our product] as they used to. But they weren't seeing what we were doing differently. The boss reminded us how two months earlier three people [workers] had died in the same month. So, he told us, he had already talked with the people of another church. He paid them some money so that they should come and do some *lamo* and over-night meetings at the workplace from today (Friday), until Sunday afternoon. He has acquired a sheep for them to slaughter here.

Coming from work, we passed some tall trees on either side of the road. As I saw those trees, they reminded me of a *wach* that I had heard from a White preacher. He was trying to teach us *weche* of medicine and healing. People did not understand him very well. He told us that "a tree is not a tree" (herbs are not medicines). To be honest, he was talking in English. It was his translator who said the *weche* above. Maybe that White man did not know that the *wach* for medicine is the same *wach* as that for a tree that grows so that you can cut it and get timbers, and medicine that you can give someone to swallow so that he recovers from his illness. He tried to show us that we should stop using medicines that we know from our forefathers. Some people were not very happy with that *wach*. Why should he want us to leave our medicine so that we purchase the White man's medicines and give them much money?

When I accompanied another friend of mine to his house, we found that he had a visitor. My friend worships in the Catholic church. His visitor also is a Catholic. But he is a Catholic who is saved. That is, in the group that is called *adundu* (heart). As we entered, my friend *lemo* for us as we were still standing. Then he told us how he is. He told us the year in which he was saved, and the date, and the time! He told us he is a sinner. Long ago he used to be adulterous, a thief, who could abuse people by insulting them. These days he walks in the sun - meaning he goes regularly to a meeting on Tuesdays early morning so as to be cleansed. That is a meeting for the confession of sins. It is led slowly. There is good teaching on the Bible at every meeting. It is of people who are *ler*. If you are not *ler* then you are removed from that meeting. Another time I have seen a *mama* who was inherited by a *jater* (widow inheritor) [a practice widely considered to be unchristian - an illicit excuse for sex outside of marriage, etc.]. She was driven away forcefully (from the meeting) - so that others learn.

Now we have reached Friday night. Saturday, as I have said above, is a day of burying many people. That means that Friday night is the night for overnight meetings at the homes of funerals. Once we reached 9.00pm, we could hear funerals in two places. On one side, they were playing a loud stereo system. On the other side they were beating drums. The people playing the stereo, they explained to me, were people of *piny*. The person being buried at that place was killed by people as he tried to steal maize from someone's home. In that other home, it is the *Nomiya* (church) people who are going to bury. Their drum will beat as they sing until morning. It must be someone who they really liked. *Roho* (spirit) gives them the strength to sing until the night is over and the dawn has broken.

Saturday

Friday night about 9.00 pm, we were surprised to find other people passing close to *dala* (our homestead) making a lot of noise. They were walking towards the funeral. Some of them were trying to sing. The *weche* (matters) that they were shouting we were not able to hear. I think many people wanted to leave their houses so as to hear what was going on.

As I thought about that *wach*, I realised that truly the Luo people like to make a noise. At the time when someone first dies, people wail. The exception is - if someone dies at night then they can delay crying out until dawn has broken. That is what is required according to the customs and traditions of the Luo. Wailing is the system used to inform villagers of what has happened. It is a way also for someone to cleanse their heart (liver). Once he has wailed loudly enough, he feels that he has peace in his heart (liver). In some places it is the women who wail the most. Amongst men just an occasional one. In other places though men can also wail if death or something else bad happens.

That is what made me think of the *weche* that are written in the first letter to Timothy in the Bible. Chapter 2 and verse one says this: "Now the first thing that I ask from you is that people take their crying out loud to God as they *lemo* (pray) and as they beseech him for all people, and give thanks." The thing that amazed me is the *wach* of *ter ywakgi* (cry out loud). That encourages the Luo to make a din to God when they want to *lemo* to him. But if you read that in another language, especially in English, it doesn't suggest that at all. That is what made me realise that translations of the Bible can take people into doing all kinds of things, even if those things weren't in their original way of life, or if they are absent in translations of the Bible into other languages.

Something else that can have people to like making a din when they *lemo* is because they think that their noise will frighten away the *jochiende* ("spirits"). Many times someone can *lemo* when he is found in some difficulty. Now he *lemo* so as to be rescued. If the difficulty is brought by *jochiende* (which happens frequently), he hopes that if he *lemo* with a loud voice the *jochiende* will be startled, will run, and will leave. Many Christians in the church like to *lemo* loudly in the name of Jesus. They realise that: there is much power in that name of Jesus.

Early in the morning on Saturday we found that many people passed by *dala* as they were coming from the funeral. They wanted to go back to their homes so as to drink their *chai*, maybe wash, and then they'd return again to the funeral for the burial (service) itself. Once dawn had broken, the music also stopped. People find time to rest before they return to the burial that starts around 11.00 hrs. Few people stayed around the funeral so as to sweep up, set out chairs and such like *weche*.

All that time the coffin is put in front of the senior wife's house in that *dala*. The coffin forms the focus for whatever happens in the funeral; there is no doubt about that at all. That is, everything happens so as to please that dead person. Before the body has been brought to the *dala* the people who have come are still few. Once the body has arrived, people start coming - many. Almost everyone who comes to the *dala* so as to be at the funeral, first goes to the coffin before going anywhere else or doing anything else. If you go to the funeral as a visitor and perhaps people aren't sure why you have come, they will show you the way to go to the coffin. Once you have reached the coffin, it needs for you first to look at the body itself. You can see because the coffin at the place of the head of the late is opened, or it may be covered only with glass. Then after that the Christians must *lemo* as they stand there.

It is not easy to know what people are *lemo* as they stand alongside the coffin. It could be that others are *lemo* for those who are gathered, or those who remain who the departed has left. But, it is easy if you stand alongside that body, for you to *lemo* for the person who has died for God to put him in a place that is good. There are some denominations in Christianity that do not see the point in *lemo* for someone who has already died. But even if someone's denomination should teach like that, it's not easy at all for people to hear. They know at those times that the person who has died still hears that which they say.

In many funerals, the coffin is put in front of where people are when they are talking. Meaning, at the time when you want to begin the burial service, it is common for the coffin to be put between the church leaders and the people, then you begin. People who testify on different things do so as they stand alongside the coffin.

Many houses that are built here in the land of the Luo, if they are the big houses of the homestead (facing down), they are built with a space in which the coffin of someone who has died can be put. Often this space resembles a verandah. But if you know the *weche* of the Luo, you realise it is not a normal verandah but somewhere for the coffin to sit.

As I was thinking about this, I found that the *chai* for the morning was already prepared. I washed, and then I began to drink *chai*.

That day we received *chai* and sweet potatoes. Sweet potatoes help people a great deal when it comes to times when food is short. They can be planted at times when other crops are not planted. Just as I wanted to put the sweet potato into my mouth, I was startled by someone's saying *"Hodi"*. "Come in", I answered. It was my friend Ralph. He came in. I welcomed him to the table.

Ralph has been my friend for many days. His name is Omondi. His father's name is Ogiro. His baptismal name is Ralph. Many people these days have a baptismal name as well as their other names. The baptismal name wants to be a Christian name, to show that the person is a follower of Jesus. So many times it is found to be a name that has come from the Bible. The name "Ralph" however does not come from the Bible. It is just a name for Whites. Many Luo people know that the name for a White person is a Christian name - so they can use any White person's name as a Christian name. That shows how the religion of Christianity amongst the Luo has taken on board the religion of the Whites. A Christian amongst the Luo is a person who tries to do things according to the customs and traditions of Whites in many ways.

I invited Ralph to my table at once, as is required to be done if a visitor comes into the house. Trying to conceal the food from him - is taken as being a bad thing. When a visitor comes as you are eating, you must welcome him (her). There is another *wach* regarding food if a visitor comes, so if you want to prepare food for him, you must put someone from the home to eat with him together, so that it be seen that they together are taking food from the one pot. This is because, if you give him his food alone, you may put poison into the food. That doesn't have to be poison as the Whites take poison - for example, arsenic - no. It could be poison that a witchdoctor has prepared for use in killing your enemy. That is, poison, the power of which comes from witchcraft.

Ralph had come to tell me some *weche* regarding the funeral of that thief. He told me that others had informed him he had gone to steal because he had been bewitched by the people of Burr. The people of Burr are another clan that live alongside the Rido river. The Burr person who had bewitched him is a *jadak* (non-paying tenant) in their *piny*, whom the brothers of Okwach (who died) had deprived of his land long ago. Ralph understood that the people of Burr killed Okwach in revenge to his grandfather who had deprived them of land. I was amazed as I heard the *wach* that he continued to tell to me. Other young men who had come from Okwach were wanting to burn the maize of the people of Burr. Ralph refused them, but it was not easy. "A Luo person does not die without reason", I said to him, Ralph. "That is so", he responded to me, "there must be someone who arranged the death of Okwach".

The truth is, a Luo person knows - he will not die. Also he does not want to die. If he dies, then there is someone who has killed him. But people keep on dying. That shows that jealous people, people with bad hearts, bitter people and killers, others of all sorts, are there! If they were not there, then people would not be dying so. This is why we say - "Witchcraft (power) is much". Although not as much as it was long ago. These days the *wach* of God has finished witchcraft - much. These days people can eat at one *kuon* (maize-meal porridge) that long ago wouldn't have been possible.

Ralph has also heard another *wach* about the death of Okwach that also he told me. The daughter of Usego was an in-law to Okwach. Her husband died two years ago. At the funeral of her husband the daughter of Usego promised in front of all the people - she would not want a *jater* (widow inheritor). But eighteen months later she was found to be pregnant. People say the person who "gave her the pregnant" had come from the people of Kamusonga. But many of the people of Kamusonga are friends of Okwach. One day recently Okwach had come to me in order to inform me of his being troubled, once he had discovered the *wach* of the pregnancy of the daughter of Usego. He met with that person of Kamusonga at another funeral. They ate together, from one *kuon*. Okwach secretly shared another *wach* with me. He has inherited that daughter of Usego herself who the person of Kamusonga that one it is said made her pregnant. But what we know here in the land of the Luo - if two people will relate sexually with a widow, but then they eat from one *kuon*, then one of them must die.

The *wach* of *jater* is a *wach* that troubles in *piny* Luo up to today. Whites do not like it even a little. I also do not like it even a little. It is said that it is the practice of *joter* that makes many Luo these days die. But they have been pressurised much to leave off those *weche*. When the husband of a woman dies, they say the woman remains with *okola*. This meaning that - that death that took hold of that husband is still with her. That means that she is not very free to move around, or do some things, or go to other places until she finds a *jater* who can cleanse her. The person who wants to be with her first is a bit of a crazy person. Meaning, someone daft enough that he can agree to sleep with a woman even if it should be for four days only, so as to remove *okola*, for her to be free. After that a woman can try in different ways (to get a *jater*) but it is necessary for him to be a brother-in-law. Another big *wach* is for him to move her into her new *dala*.

Starting a new *dala* is a very big *wach*. I will not be able to explain all *weche* connected with it here! But what happens is that if someone's son gets to be able to walk carrying an axe, it is taken that those people are ready to start a new *dala*. The senior man first looks for advice from a witchdoctor. Then he takes a cock, and ties it up at the location where he wants to start the new *dala*. If the next day the chicken has already been killed, that shows that location is not good for his new *dala*. But if he finds that it is still alive, that shows that the place is appropriate for a new *dala*. Then he wants to leave the old homestead with his senior wife, his first born son, and other things so that he can prepare the place to stay that will in turn be the place for his children, until his sons begin to start their own *dala*.

Now if a woman does not have a husband, according to the Luo traditions, she cannot start a new *dala*, which forces her to stay in the *dala* of her father-in-law. There she can not be very free. Also this does not allow her sons good opportunity to build their houses. She cannot be considered a senior woman while she is still in the *dala* of her father-in-law. She is still under the ruling of her father-in-law. In order to start a new home, she must get a man. *Jater* are the men who will agree to help widows in this way. A *jater* agrees to live with a widow in her house. While he is there, she must look after him. She can use that new man, in order to have her new *dala* made. Many women, once they have their new *dala*, they chase away that man. He then can go and look for another widow so as to help her in that way.

Joter these days are really dying. It is a work that has a lot of hazards. Moving someone's *dala* is not an easy thing. It is easy for *chira* to take a hold of people who are starting new homes. People fear that work. But still people can also be found to do it. These days they say it is the disease of "I plunder you" (AIDS) that is killing people. AIDS though, I am perceiving, resembles *chira*.

The time came when I was wanting to go to the funeral. Ralph by this time had already left. The mother of the house was still busy in the kitchen. I started out. I went alone. We cannot go with my wife together. People around here do not walk with their wives. If you did this, others would think you think too highly of yourself. Then jealousy takes hold of them; they bewitch you.

As I neared the place of the funeral, I noticed that Okwach's land

22

was bounded by *ojuok*. *Ojuok* is a singular kind of bush. It does not resemble other plants. Maybe that is why it is used to show the border between one plot and another. Its name also always amazes me. It is called, as I said above, *ojuok*. "*Juok*" though is also the name given to the hearts (livers) of people who have died. Now I think that it was chosen the name for that bush so that people should fear removing the *ojuok* that has been put there by the elders. On the other hand maybe you can say - people chose a plant with a frightening name to show where the border is?

Okwach had by that time already started his new *dala*. He did not start the new *dala* in the way that the forefathers liked. He did not start by tying up a chicken and then seeing if the chicken is still alive. The reason he did not do this, that I heard, is because that would show that he still believed in the gods of our forefathers: it is the power of *juogi* that would result in the chicken either surviving or dying. This is why these days many Christians do not want to tie up a cock as people used to do long ago.

That which brought Okwach a big *wach*, is because he started his new *dala* in the absence of the senior wife. He did this, according to the *weche* I got from people, because death came unexpectedly to the woman the day before he had planned to start the new home. People said and the mother of the children also agreed that he go ahead starting his new *dala* even in the absence of the senior wife because they believed the blood of Jesus would cover them. So the old man Okwach started his new *dala* while the mother of the children was (away) at a funeral. Later *wach* became very difficult! The friends as also the neighbours of Okwach couldn't agree either with Okwach's wife or with Okwach himself. They shocked the wife to Okwach when they told her that if she went into that new *dala* then she would die! And they continued to pull each other back and fore on that *wach* for many days. Okwach refused to go back and start another *dala*. Instead of doing so, he arranged for a goat to be sacrificed so as to finish that *dhoch*. The goat was killed but still the senior wife feared a great deal. In the end, it forced him to make for the senior wife another *dala*, so that he had two *dala* - the big *dala* where the young wife was and the small *dala* where the senior wife stayed.

That was still just difficult. When it came for the time for the children to build, it became even more difficult. The children did not want to build in their mother's home (senior mother), but they wanted to build together in the *dala* at once - where the junior wife was, as they continued to encourage their mother that she stay in her house that is in the big *dala* that she refused point blank to do. These *weche* troubled the heart (liver) of Okwach for a long time.

That big *dala* of Okwach was surrounded by different kinds of trees. Because the old man had died outside, they broke a gap into the surrounding trees so as to take the body in. It is said (*wach*) - if someone dies outside of the *dala* then he must be brought in by breaking the fence. He is not taken in through the gate. That is the law that people of long ago have left us. Rules like that Christians attack every day. But in some places people still just do them because they do fear.

This *dala* was arranged as all *dala* in Luoland are arranged; except that this *dala* was still new. The sons of Okwach had already started building their homes on either side below the houses of their mothers that are at the top. Four houses had already been built, two on the left and two on the right. All those houses are facing into the middle of the *dala*, laid out according to the order of birth of the sons concerned. Three houses seemed to be well looked after. One house though was very dirty and had started to fall down. That is the house of the third son, who the accident of the bus killed four years ago. Once he had been buried, his wife ran away and married (cooked) somewhere else.

At the top were two houses of the two mothers facing down. Those two houses were of the same largeness. Okwach did not want to bring jealousy between his wives. Only that one of the houses was empty and no-one was living in it, but the other the younger wife was occupying. The coffin holding the body of Okwach was in front of the house of the senior mother. It was opened so that anyone who went could see Okwach - to give him a goodbye (wish him to be kept by God). Any time when visitors to the funeral entered, they stood in front of the coffin, and then they *lemo*. Some of them would sing first. The song that they really liked there was "Amazing grace ...".

Once I had *lemo* at the body, I came back and sat down. I sat with some of my fellow elders. I did not have any particular job to do at this funeral. This is because although Okwach stayed near to me, I do not have any blood relationship with him. That is, he comes from a different door (clan) than I do. We can intermarry with his people. Truthfully - I am his in-law (my family has married one or more daughters of his family). That shows that I did not want to be there as the funeral went ahead. But that is a *wach* that I did not want to take notice of. They also knew that, that is why not they welcomed me to another house to eat special food as the law would stipulate!

The church wanting to bury today is CCA. That stands for Church of Christ in Africa that is also called *johera* (people of love). That is a church that separated out from Anglican of Kenya in 1957. They are one church that emphasises strongly on funerals. They see that it is at funerals that they meet with many different people, and it is where they can find new members if they do well at the funeral. Things that are taken as good - are like parading with the coffin, dancing, stepping, dressing well, showing people love, etc. etc.

After arranging the chairs, the leaders of CCA started leading the meeting. Their leaders sat in front of us wearing their priestly clothes. They first go with young men who can carry the coffin to the main house. They stand around the coffin then they come with it walking in procession, and again they sing. Then they put the coffin on the small table that has already been put there.

Once this has been done, opportunity was now given for those who were wanting to speak on *weche* concerning the deceased. The names of people were already written on a piece of paper, for them to be called one by one so as to give whatever testimony they have. The truth is - that many people come to the funeral wanting to hear those *weche* more than other *weche*. Often you will find that *weche* at someone's death that you did not know all the days that he was alive. Really - people want to assess according to how the people testifying talk, *weche* of the heart or hearts (livers) of the village. As already mentioned above - no one dies without cause. There must be something that has killed him. Not something like an accident, illness, war or people who are fighting. No. Something that comes from someone's heart (liver) - should that person be alive or should they be dead. Therefore a funeral is a place for assessing the hearts (livers) of people. If you keep going to many funerals you begin to realise how the heart (liver) of the village, "family", or *dala* resembles.

The funeral of Okwach had many difficult *weche*. First it was a police case as he was murdered/slaughtered. Secondly many people asked themselves - did he really go there to steal? If he did not go there to steal, then what did he go there to do? Those who were standing for him tried to answer those questions as best they could. In the end though it was clear to see - there was no person who could see that matter well. Perhaps he went so as to commit adultery with some woman or girl - but that girl was not coming forward to confess if that had been his intention. So it remained a question or a hidden *wach* that was yet to be revealed.

Many of the *weche* that are there are not said openly in front of the people. But they are *weche* that people whisper amongst themselves. Many of those *weche* it is women who are aware of. Perhaps their husbands will learn about them once they have returned to their homes. Others are *weche* that the men knew very well - but don't talk about as do the women. Even *weche* that are known by men; women are most likely to speak them out.

Testifying can take two hours or more. After that the *wach* is returned into the hands of the church. The church people have preachers. Frequently when the preacher stands up to preach the *wach* of God, is the time when people begin to not have peace. People can be that they start whispering and talking to one another. Others stand up and leave. Others are welcomed to the food. (Others begin to invite visitors to eat even while the testifiers are still speaking.) Because people are many, and many of them want to eat, they cannot all eat at once when the funeral is over. Therefore people are invited to eat slowly by slowly as the meeting goes on.

As people started talking, I heard as three people were talking in front of me. "Do you think it is *chira* that kills people these days?" asked one person. "It is 'I plunder you' (AIDS)", the second responded. "'I plunder you', is that not the same as *chira?*" someone else asked. They were quiet for a while. "'I plunder you' is not *chira*; 'I plunder you' is a disease that was brought by the Whites", the third person told them. "If the Whites brought 'I plunder you', what happened to *chira?*" the second person replied to him. "*Chira* these days does not have power as it did long ago?" the first person asked. "Right", was the response of the third person. "So then long ago it was *chira* that was killing people", the first person *wacho* "But these days it is 'I plunder you'?" "That is so", the third person answered him. "But where is the difference between *chira* and 'I plunder you'?" the first person asked. "Yes", the second person added, as he really wanted an answer to that question. "None really", the third person *wacho*. "Maybe the name

'I plunder you' is likely to startle us more than the *wach* of *chira*?"
Then they were quiet.

I was amazed as I heard that conversation between one girl and
two boys that were around 30 years old. I was amazed how the
Whites these days have confused us. Children stay at school for many
years, but what they are taught in school has no foundation. What is
said at school, is far from what happens in the *dala*, in the family,
in their houses ... They cannot understand *wach* deeply. They only
knew that "I plunder you" is a translation of AIDS. But they could not
realise that something resembling 'I plunder you' could come without
something else except that a virus enters into their body. They know
that sin (breaking taboo) brings *chira*. They have been told that the sin
of adultery brings *chira*. Therefore those two *weche* are similar. *Chira*
comes if you break the laws of our ancestors. "I plunder you" comes
if you break the laws of our forefathers also but the Whites have also
added their laws, and they emphasise other laws.

(*Chira* is a disease that makes someone weak, thin, and then to
die. It happens to someone who does not have respect for the dead.
The Luo tend to have many laws that someone needs to follow in
order to avoid *chira* from taking a hold of him.)

Weche of funerals generally don't go ahead without troublesome
issues. Frequently a funeral has a drunkard or madman who wants to
trouble. This funeral was of that ilk. The troubler of *weche* funeral at
this funeral was a mad man who lived close to the home of Okwach.
Whenever someone wanted to speak, or sing, or do something else,
that mad man began his games. An old man castigated him sharply.
Then he led him by his hands so as to take him away from there. But
that person came back, and came back again, and came back again.
When the preacher was preaching he troubled again. The preacher
refuted him in the name of Jesus for him to leave off, to be quiet.
But he carried on.

Something that makes people to fear a mad person, is their thinking that a mad man is a person who is led by *jochiende*. Madness is not some deficiency in the mind of a person, no. It is someone who is full of *jochiende* in his heart (liver) and that lead him into doing *weche* that are daft. That is the reason people fear a mad person more than others.

Sunday

At the time when *piny* (the world) was wanting to break into light, the sound of a vehicle was heard as it entered into a neighbouring *dala*. Some children went straight away so as to see what was happening. A boy, a son of that *dala*, had already got very sick. His wife died two years ago. At night the illness got worse. Now they had come to collect him to take him to hospital.

People have already talked much about the *wach* that has brought him that disease. When the senior wife was still alive, then we were surprised to find that one day he came with a new wife. He built her a house straight away. *Weche* were very difficult in the *dala* as the ladies competed. In the end, as the boy was in Nairobi at his job, his sisters went to there. They argued loudly (strongly) with the second wife. She ran away, she left, and we've yet to see her again. That shows that the boy was not living a *ler* life. In Nairobi he was living in a house by himself. After finishing work, for him to come back and cook his own food - was not easy.

That boy was a boy of *lemo*. One day some years ago we were surprised to find that he came to visit us wearing a long greyish-purple prayer-gown. We were amazed. He explained to us what had happened, as he had a rosary around his neck and a cross in his hand. God had called him to *lemo* for people. He himself had begun to be amazed how when he *lemo* for them they were healed. One day he *lemo* for a widow in Nairobi. She was healed in an amazing way. Then the people of the house (family) of the *mama*, and she herself, they gave him a lot of wealth. He realised the gift he had of *lamo* for the sick. Some months had now passed in which every time he was busy travelling in the work of *lamo*.

I myself I did not see how he *lemo* for people in those days. But from long ago I had realised that he was a man of *lemo*. He was able to practice *tako* - cutting someone and then sucking out the witchcraft. Younger mothers it was that I saw that went to him a great deal; he welcomed them into the house of his father. That is where he was able to take hold of someone sick - whether a child or an adult - in order to cut the skin of his/her abdomen and then to remove medicine that had been put there by the person with evil eye.

The vehicle went with him. That *wach* but was difficult. We all knew - that he had few days left. Maybe he could die even today. If someone is taken to hospital in that way, that shows that the illness has already overcome them. What the hospital will do for someone who is on the verge of death also I do not think. Someone who is sick, people fear. Our people like to go where there is a corpse. But we do not like to go to someone who is sick. People fear someone who is sick. That is why one day another *mama* showed me - if someone is sick so that they cannot walk, well then they will die. People who are very sick many of them are ostracised. People fear being haunted. If you go once someone has already died, that has no *wach*. But someone who is sick has much pain. If he sees you going to him, he will desire that you help him, that you save him. Someone who is sick though can finish much money on treatment. Sometimes what you would do is hard to know. But you, who go to visit him, he can think that you despise him because you do not help him. So it is you that he can haunt once he has died. That is why people fear (respect) someone who has died a great deal.

That day the boy died en route as they were taking him to the hospital. Once we had all heard *wach* of that death, we went all to the *dala*. People were already filling the place. Many people, more especially ladies, were wailing and crying out loudly. "God has taken him", or "He has finished his journey", people were saying. "Death is something that God ordained for it to be", another person said. If it is God who has decided the day of death of someone, and how he will die - why should his fellow (mere) people try to rescue him from that death?

I returned to the house so as to continue to prepare myself to go to *lemo*. The time was wanting to be late. The children and the mother of the house were also busy in preparing themselves. Me but today I was not going to the normal church, because my child who had been welcomed into MERCY (a place for looking after orphans).

About two years ago a friend of mine of long standing came to visit me. He had been for many days (without my seeing him). We sat down. He told me the *wach* that he had. First he asked me about my children. A little I was wanting to be startled. It is not easy for someone to ask you anything in detail about your children. People fear doing that, because it is easy to be seen as a jealous person who wants to you injure your children as his continue to do well. That is an amazing *wach* in this our *piny*. The *wach* of jealousy. What we know is that if someone wants to know how your business or your children are going, the reason is so that he can put you down. That is what makes many people lie on those *weche* so that they not be bewitched. It is easy for someone to say that he has nothing when his wealth is very much.

Shortly though I realised what this person wanted of my children. He had been sent by that organisation that helps children who are orphans, or children who are troubled. They wanted children one hundred and thirty. He showed me that, and he showed me the *ler* of a paper that he had so that I know the truth of the *wach*. He wanted to know if I had a child who they could help. I tried to show him that my children weren't troubled ones much. But he showed me, if I was able to give him one girl, the good one he was seeing was my daughter who had seven years, people will be able to give me help not a little. What they want is just $10.00.

When I thought of the things that could help that my child Rose, I was not able to refuse. Even should I not have wanted to do this, but the mother of the children once she had discovered what was happening could not be happy if I refuse people from helping a child to whom we had given birth in this way. I gave that person his money. He filled the form, and then later he took the girl into that organisation. Today is the day of parents in the church that takes the lead in the *weche* of that organisation. It is a must that I go, because my child is in it.

Sometimes *wach* of orphan children is not just so easy. There are many people who like to move around and broadcast incredible *weche* about orphan children. They can come, they take the name of children and money, then they get lost completely with the money and are not seen again. People like that have frequently deceived us in the church.

Because it is the day for *lemo*, it was not required for that my daughter to wear the clothes of the project. But there were other good clothes that her Whites had bought for her in the days of Christmas that she wore. My other children stared at her with those fine clothes. I left the house when my child had already been long gone.

There is something that the Whites call "reformed theology". For some of their churches this theology is very important. This is why there are some churches in Africa that operate with that theology.

33

They learned from the Whites. Also they take a firm hold of it so as to continue to receive assistance from those Whites. The church I am going to today is a church that the Whites stand with a great deal. But it is hard for our people to discern what is good in that teaching. That is because our people go to *lemo* so that they receive blessing. The God of the Luo does not know *weche* of reformed. He knows that if someone is made to suffer, that is because of the sin (breaking of taboo) that he has done. If someone gets wealth then he can deceive people, as if he is someone good who God blesses. I say to people, God can give blessing because of the love that he has in his heart and not because of someone's good acts - but it is not easy for them to agree with this.

Now I go to *lemo* in the church that deceives itself it is Whites. That deception brings them much profit. The Whites like them, work with them, give them other things, welcome them to visit their homes at times, and so on and so on. That deception is not only found in church. Also in all kinds of organisations. It seems that this does not trouble the Whites themselves very much. Even more than that - they are happy with it. If they see others wanting to use their language, follow their customs and traditions, eat their food, wear their clothes and use their money - that doesn't trouble them.

We started by singing a song of the book. That was difficult, because only few people have their books. Many people could not sing well. For a church to have (song) books to hand out is difficult; as books quickly get lost. For everyone to buy their own book is also difficult, also for them to remember to come with their books. Sometimes though they can sing songs of the head (that have been learned by heart), that makes everyone sing together with joy.

At the time when the preacher wants to preach, it resembled that fire caught hold of a boy in the church. He was a young boy, who just the other day got married. His wife has not yet given birth.

"Amen, alleluja, amen", he said after the preacher. The *wach* found a place in his heart. He was happy with the preacher. Suddenly and unexpectedly he began to sing. The preacher started. He stopped preaching. Many people started whispering *wach*. Then people started singing with him together, until the song finished. Once the singing had finished, then the preacher went ahead. Starting a song when someone is preaching is the practice of some churches, but it is something that this church has not yet got used to. Many people were amazed, but the *lemo* went ahead.

Later people were even more shocked. The very person began to cry out loudly. Once he had begun so to cry, he ran - half standing and half kneeling, heading for in front of the altar. Just there just there just there he hit his knees *piny* as he cried out loud and tears streamed from his eyes. He was there as he cried out to God with his loud (strong) voice. He confessed many sins of different kinds. Tears continued to flow from his eyes, and water (a wet patch) could be seen in front of him that had come from his mouth and his eyes.

Many people in the church now were amazed. Worry-someness filled their eyes. The teachers (leaders) of the church were wanting to whisper something amongst themselves. One of the elders of the church went there so as to encourage that person. "Be quiet", he told him. But he refused to be quiet. Another person a woman who was sitting near to the altar started *lemo* loudly as she wanted to chase away the *jachien* (devil) in the name of Jesus. Then we saw that two of the teachers of the church that were there on the altar had already decided what they were going to do. They went up to that person, then they took hold of him one on this side and one on that side on his arms. Then they began to pull him by force between all the people who were sitting there, half carrying him, until they removed him out of the church, then they took him into another house so that his crying not trouble people who were in the church.

It could be that some others were startled by the actions of that person. But others couldn't have been very surprised. The type of *lemo* which that person showed happens every day in other churches. Sometimes those churches are called churches of power because they believe very much in the power of God. In the everyday *lemo*, once the preacher has preached sufficiently, the people *lemo* just begin to cry out loud. First they cry while sitting on their chairs. But later, after some more seconds or minutes, they begin to run leaving their chairs behind but going to kneel in front of where the preacher is standing. Then they can stay there for up to 15 minutes as they continue to cry out loud. Others who are there can chase some *jochiende* away from them. Sometimes those who are *lemo* for the *jochiende* to leave may be around five people. Some people are held as they are *lemo* for, should they want to jump, run or bump into people with their arms or head. The time taken to *lemo* for the person who has *jochiende* could be another 10 minutes. Then that person is quiet (and comes back to their normal senses). That is the kind of *lemo* that this person is used to, therefore he did it even in this church on this Sunday, where there are different kinds of people mixed up who are not used to such practices.

When the time had come for announcements, they stood up one another *mama* who is one of the leaders of that church so as to open up to us another *wach*. *Mama* confessed what had happened to her one week previously. She apologised (*wach mos*) because she was not in church the previous week, but she had not shown people that she wouldn't be there, but the *wach* that took hold of her came to her unexpectedly. She measured out to us how she had heard the *wach* of the death of her grandchild (a grandchild of one of her sisters). It forced her to follow along with that sister so that they follow up the *wach* of the boy who died together with her. When they had reached Nairobi, they discovered that boy who was called Oboro had been killed because he was found wanting to steal the bike of someone that he had left alongside a shop. But as they went to the police they were shown that the corpse is not in Nairobi, but they must go to Naivasha. Because it was Friday, they hung out in Nairobi until Monday, then they were able to get travel money then they went to Naivasha. The next day they went back to Naivasha again. Later once the people of the mortuary had completed their busyness, they entered and they saw a corpse other that truly had been badly burnt. It was difficult for them to know whether truly that was Oboro or not. But another sister on seeing his wrist saw that he had worn a bracelet of some sort, and his wrist had burned differently where the metal was than where there was no metal. That is why she thought that it must be him. The grandmother to the child touched him. At the time that she touched him blood came out of his eyes on both sides, and also out of the sides of his mouth. That is what made her know that he was her grandson truly; he cried when he realised that it was his grandma who had touched him.

At the time when the meeting was wanting to end, we were surprised to find another lady standing. She went so as to be in front of the people before the altar, as another *mama* also accompanied her to there. I did not hear that she had been invited to go there, but it appears that she just went. No-one stopped her either. When she had arrived, after she had led people in a song, she started talking. She talked with courage and with vigour as a person who knew the *wach* that they wanted to *wacho* very clearly. She spoke to us on *weche* of spirit and *weche* of salvation. She encouraged us that we should be filled with the Holy Spirit. She showed us she wanted for us to receive the gift of talking in many languages. She measured to us how the Spirit of God wants to heal people, if they would only believe in him (accept him). She called people so that they should go forward and should go up to her. But no other person went. Instead of doing that, all the people just stayed there as they were very silent and looked at her. Afterwards when she had already sat down the leader of the service finished the service for us so that people could return to their homes. Two weeks later I heard that the *mama* and her people had been chased away from the church. Then they started their church nearby. There are churches that refuse *weche* of spirit.

The people of MERCY also they spoke. They told us about how many children nowadays they are helping. They made themselves out to be very clever to be able to help even children of people who are able (i.e. not very poor). They opened to us how MERCY was giving the church much wealth. They encouraged us for us to come to a meeting other where the Whites will be, so that we have them know how we are happy with the assistance they are sending, also how poverty is still troubling us and we want in order to them to add sending us more help. They warned us that should we have some complaints about the *wach* of the project we should not give those complaints at the times the Whites are there.

After *lemo* as I was wanting to get nearer to *dala*, I heard a drum being beaten in another *dala* nearby. When I turned my ear carefully, I realised it was the drum of *Nomiya* (church). It is the *Nomiya* people who have a singular way of *lemo*. Some *weche* they take from Muslims, for example men who are leaders want in order to be circumcised. Many of the *weche* also come from Christianity. Many of the *Nomiya* though emphasise the faith of the Old Testament. They like to say "God is one". They see Jesus as a prophet. They permit men to marry many wives.

I decided to go and meet up with them at the memorial service. They were remembering an elder who had died last year, together with some of his family who had died in an accident four years ago. Sometimes they can go to someone's *dala* in that way so as to perform a celebration (ritual) for more than one person who died long ago. I found them as they were in that *dala* as they were gathering under a tarpaulin. The elders of the church stayed in front of me, having put on their amazing clothes that carry all kinds of different colours that were shining *ler*.

By that time they had ceased to sing and beat the drum. I found that the preacher had begun his work, but that some sons of the *dala* were wanting to trouble (him). It was difficult for the leaders of the church to know what to do as they were in the *dala* of other people. The owners of the *dala* were having difficulty as they tried to prevent the young men so that they not destroy the *weche* that were going forward. Then I saw some young men come and take hold of the noise-maker by force; they took him into another house in an adjoining *dala*, and closed the door on him.

After a few *weche*, all the people started to walk together, with the people of the home leading the procession, as they sung loudly, beat the drums and blew the (home-made) horn. We went nearly everybody up to the gate of the *dala* and then we returned to behind the houses where some people had previously been buried. Those graves had already been covered in white sheets, one on this side on the grave of the old man and others on the other side on those other graves. Now people began to walk around those graves, as they were still singing. Afterwards they removed those sheets. Later on a craftsman came in order to cover the graves in a good way with cement.

In a memorial service, a cow must be slaughtered. Many of our people would agree that until something has been slaughtered, a celebration cannot be good or satisfying ('sweet'). That made me think of some *weche* concerning another brother in Christ. He agreed to provide food for the funeral of one of his fathers (uncles). Once he had been told how many people would be there who would want to eat, he went in order to buy more than sufficient meat in a shop. The people of that *dala* they refused that meat completely! What they wanted, they *wacho*, is a cow to be slaughtered in the *dala*. Not meat that has been purchased in a shop. That is like a *wach* that happens when a visitor visits another *dala*. The residents of the *dala* will desire to shed blood for the visitor. If they just buy meat, that will not satisfy them. Often times what is easy to slaughter for a visitor is a chicken. If the visitor is big (important) or they are many - they will slaughter for them a sheep or goat.

After spending some time at the memorial service, a *wach* was sent to say that my daughter had come to *dala*, I should try to go and talk with her because she has some difficult *weche*. After staying on a little longer, I set off for home.

Once I had reached home, I found *migogo*. *Migogo* is the name given to a girl once she has gone to cook (been married) if she returns to her home-place (birthplace). It is not a good name. That is so as to deter girls from being too quick to come back. Being a *migogo* is difficult as there is no respect (fear) she can get when she is at her home in that way. A neighbour of ours another year *migogo* went up to him with a little child. There were many *weche* at her husband's home. After a few months that boy child died. All that time, she would sleep on the dirt on the floor in the kitchen of her mother. It is not permitted for her (*migogo*) to sleep in any other house. That girl continued to grow more and more sick, until also she died. The people of her husband did not come even to visit her. She went (originally) by eloping. Bride-wealth was still to be paid. At the funeral, some of the people from the home of the boy came. She was buried outside of the *dala*. *Migogo* cannot be buried with respect in the (confines of the) *dala*. She must be buried outside (the fence). Like someone who is discarded or despised.

My daughter greeted me. We sat together with people of the home and other visitors. People were many. Afterwards once the visitors had gone, I went to sit outside under a tree, then my daughter came to me and sat besides me. My heart (liver) was paining from the *weche* difficult that she was receiving. First she had got pregnant while in school. Her child died. He was a boy. The second time she cooked for someone (was married by someone) who was a self made "engineer" on the side of the road in Kisumu. That person had two wives, and his (girl)friends were many. She came back to *dala* before she had given birth. Her heart (liver) was troubling her enormously. The boy whom she had gone to cook for had yet to pay bride-wealth for her. A wedding will not be possible as she is not the senior wife. The man said he will come to collect her. But we know he won't come. He has promised to do so very often, and doesn't do it (i.e. does not come). He does not care. Why should he care about my daughter, as he has many wives?

In the afternoon I took her to my friend who is a pastor. Also he talked with her. He warned her and castigated her strongly. My daughter, tears filled her eyes. Then he *lemo* for her strongly (loudly), as my daughter had knelt down before him as tears flowed from her eyes. She continued crying quietly. Then later she began to wail as she cried out loudly (strongly). She fell down, and began to turn around this way and that way. The pastor continued to castigate her loudly as he chased away the *jachien* in the name of Jesus. She laid down and rested. She stood up so as to remove the dust that had taken hold of her clothes. We gave thanks to my friend. I returned her to the *dala* now having been cleansed. My daughter loves the *Wach* of God a great deal. She continued to stay with me in the *dala* for two months. Then one day in the afternoon she didn't come back. She had already gone to be married by someone else. I *lemo* for her for God to help her this time around.

I agree that on the side of children things these days are difficult. If they are not saved so that salvation gives them perseverance in adversity, it is easy for them to fall into many difficult *weche*. Long ago the old men used to look after their children so that for a girl to get pregnant before getting married was very difficult. She knew that if that was to happen, it would be to her great embarrassment. In the end it was arranged for her to be married by an old man who already had more wives. A girl who was "easy to get" was much despised. These days but it is not like that. There is much grace. A girl can get pregnant while in school, but just goes ahead with her studies as the grandma looks after child for her. Many of the children who come to be in that way die though. Maybe they realize - they are there, but they are not wanted.

Things like this could not have happened long ago. The Whites when they came they undermined the power of the elders. These days they have no power. People who can give instructions to children and in order for them to hear it is hard to find. The church tries. But the church also, it seems as if it has no teeth. It has been bought by the Whites. The church is busy *lamo* for money that comes from outside, and also it is involved in the *weche* and troubles of the Whites. They don't have much opportunity or reason for them to trouble themselves painfully in *weche* that are not so as to get money from overseas. What gain is there in that?

That night we ate in silence. I was happy because my daughter was there. I was happy because she had been *lemo* for. She had been cleansed. *Weche* but many were on me heavy. Where are my people heading? We go ahead with our *weche* that come from our forefathers as far as it is possible. We arrange memorial services and funerals to be as impressive as can be. We know doing many of the things that the Whites do. There are even some that we show off to say that we know more than the Whites themselves! But sometimes it is as if in everything, they are ahead and we are behind. Things that we take as valuable these days all come from their place. Ours remains to try and follow their customs and traditions from a great distance. Because their *weche* come with money, there is no point in doing anything else. God to help us.

www.ingramcontent.com/pod-product-compliance
Lightning Source LLC
Chambersburg PA
CBHW072038060426
42449CB00010BA/2328